mission
ACCOMPLISHED

ROBERT AND METTA SILLIMAN'S
MISSIONARY WORK
IN THE PHILIPPINES,
1924-1966

People working together make a difference to the world!

Tawny Ryan Nelb

TAWNY RYAN NELB

Published by Tawny Ryan Nelb and the Bertha E. R. Strosacker Memorial Presbyterian Church, Midland, Michigan, 2012

Nelb, Tawny Ryan
Mission Accomplished: Robert and Metta Silliman's Missionary Work in the Philippines, 1924-1966 / Tawny Ryan Nelb
Includes bibliographical references and index
ISBN-13: 978-0615531304
ISBN-10: 061553130X

This book is printed on acid-free paper.

A best faith effort was made to contact all copyright holders.

Images on Front Cover: background photograph shows hills and forests around Casala-an, 2008, where Sillimans hid 1942-1944, Courtesy Frederick Dael; postcard and photo of Silliman Institute, 1923 and Robert and Metta Silliman, c late 1960s, Courtesy The Herbert H. and Grace A. Dow Foundation; First Presbyterian Church postcard, c 1912, Courtesy Tawny Ryan Nelb.

Visit www.amazon.com, www.nelbarchival.com, or www.createspace.com/3635869 to order additional copies

Dedicated to the members of the
Bertha E. R. Strosacker Memorial Presbyterian
Church congregation and their stalwarts
of the church's history:
Ellis (Ned) Brandt,
Ralph and Jean Hillman,
and Dorothy Langdon Yates

List of Figures

Preface and Acknowledgments:

The Bertha E. R. Strosacker Memorial Presbyterian Church (hereafter Memorial Presbyterian Church) of Midland, Michigan has been actively engaged in the local community and the world at large, including missionary work, for over one hundred years. This booklet will tell the story of a forty year collaboration between one of the Presbyterian Church's long time members, Grace Anna Ball Dow, missionaries Robert and Metta Silliman, Silliman University in the Philippines, and members of the Memorial Presbyterian Church (whose congregation attended the First Presbyterian Church in the early days) in Midland. The story is based on the historical documents at the church, at the Presbyterian Historical Society in Philadelphia, Pennsylvania, and at the Herbert H. and Grace A. Dow Foundation where records of the Dow family are held. Additional records were saved by Dorothy Wilson and the church (Silliman Collection #68) and donated to the Foundation by Ralph Hillman.

This monograph was inspired by the author's research on the life and legacy of Grace Dow and an exhibit assembled by Christina Westbury, then the Reference Coordinator for the Post Street Archives. At the request of church member, Marilyn Wildes, the author prepared and presented (October 30, 2007) a lecture on Grace Dow and the Sillimans for the congregation of the Memorial Presbyterian Church. After the lecture, congregation members, Ned Brandt and Ralph Hillman, expressed an interest in seeing it published for distribution to other church members. The author transformed the lecture into publishable text and added significant additional resources.

The author is most grateful for the contributions of Metta and Robert Silliman's foster children in the Philippines: Emma Cole Teves, Eleanor Funda-Sardual, and Frederick S. Dael and his daughter, Metta Dael, in Massachusetts, especially for Fred Dael's significant assistance facilitating access to copyright permission for several images.

Thanks, too, are due Margaret Ann Riecker, Jenee Velasquez, and Pat Albrecht of the Herbert H. and Grace A. Dow Foundation for use of important images, the Reverend Dr. David Pierce and Linda Baker for use of historical images in the Memorial Presbyterian Church archives, the Presbyterian Historical Society in Philadelphia for use of their images and other documents, to past colleagues Ellis (Ned) Brandt, Dana Fey, Kathy McCormick, and Delores Goulet, and the Memorial Presbyterian Church's past and present Mission Interpretation and Stewardship committee members Susan Asher, Norm Donker, Rick Drimalla, Bill Krueger, Bill Lauderbach, Elsie Misner, Tracy Perry, Susan Putnam, Glenn Stuart, Andy Thompson, and especially Mark Maxwell and Ralph Hillman for their support, patience, and perseverance as we worked through the logistics of getting the booklet edited and published.

The author also thanks the Reverend Dr. David Robertson for his support. Special thanks go to Ellamarie Schroeder for reading the book and suggesting editorial changes. Her thorough review made it a better book. Most importantly thanks to my spouse Robert G. Nelb for the clarity of his editorial eye and his unwavering support for all my publication projects.

Although this narrative only recounts the work of Robert and Metta Silliman and a few of the many dedicated men and women who contributed to the growth and development of Silliman University and the Presbyterian Church in Midland over the years, it is an amazing story about how collaboration among people and commitment to others can have a worldwide impact.

Tawny Ryan Nelb, January 2012

§§§

Robert and Metta Silliman's missionary work in the Philippines is mostly due to their great faith, their love of the Filipino people, and their perseverance through both joyful and difficult times. But support for their work is, at least in part, a result of a serendipitous intersection of people, places, and institutions that came together in Midland, Michigan. Midland, today a medium size community of 42,000 people in the middle of Michigan's Lower Peninsula, grew from a centuries-old meeting place of the Anishinabe (Saginaw Chippewa) Indians at the confluence of the Chippewa and Tittabawassee Rivers. An influx of European-American settlers looking for a new life in the 19th century brought hunters and then farmers, lumbermen, and the businesses that grew to serve their needs and allowed the community to prosper.

Charlotte Ewers Ball Woodbury, known as Grandma Ball, was one of those pioneers who came to Midland, Michigan in 1861 from Massachusetts to live with her son, hotelier and later farmer, George Fordyce Ball. Charlotte was a co-founder of the original Presbyterian Church in Midland in 1867.[1] The first church building was built in 1868 at the northwest corner of Townsend and Larkin Streets. Later, in 1878, her grandson, Benjamin B. Ball, became a member and trustee of the First Presbyterian Church (a position he held for twenty-one years). His wife, Minnie Warner Ball, was an active member and leader among the church women's groups for at least seven decades.

Charlotte's great-granddaughter, Grace Anna Ball Dow, born in 1869, grew up in the town. Although Charlotte and other relatives had been involved in the Presbyterian Church early on, Grace's immediate family was a member of the St. John's Episcopal Church just a block away on Larkin Street. Although she did not officially join until 1923, Grace's direct involvement in the Presbyterian Church began in 1892 when she married Herbert H. Dow, a Clevelander who had joined the First Presbyterian Church in 1890 when he moved to Midland to form the Midland Chemical Company and The Dow Chemical Company several years later. He transferred his membership from the Methodist Episcopal Church in Canton, Ohio where he had been working on another start-up, the Canton Chemical Company.[2]

FIGURE 1.
Charlotte Ewers Ball Woodbury
(Grandma Ball), c 1870s,
Courtesy of The Memorial Presbyterian Church
Archives.

FIGURE 2.
Grace Ball Dow, c 1892,
of The Herbert H.
and Grace A. Dow
Foundation.

FIGURE 3.
Herbert H. Dow, c 1888,
Courtesy of The Herbert
H. and Grace A. Dow
Foundation.

FIGURE 4.
The Dow's Church, First Presbyterian Church, the congregation's
second church building built in 1882, postcard, c 1912, Courtesy
of Tawny Ryan Nelb.

Over time, and with the growth and success of The Dow Chemical Company, Herbert and Grace Dow made significant contributions to the First Presbyterian Church. The first concrete sidewalk to replace the old pine planks in 1901, paint for the church and manse, carpeting, pew cushions, and repairs to the organ were gifts made to the First Presbyterian Church along with their yearly subscription of financial support.[3] Six of the Dow's seven children went to Sunday school and were confirmed in the church.[4] Both Herbert and Grace were involved with various boards and groups within the church. Herbert was a church Trustee, and Grace belonged to several women's groups including the Abbey Circle and both Foreign and Home Missionary Societies where she filled day-to-day and leadership roles over many years.[5] Her work with the women's groups was typical of church women of her time.

Women's groups were very important in the Presbyterian Church, not only for their financial and time commitments within their specific area of interest, but also to provide a social network and a way for the women to influence church policy through their husbands at a time when women had neither a vote nor a place at the table within church administrative affairs. The women's Missionary Society, organized in 1884, was one such group and became the bulwark for church missionary activities such as educating the congregation about the religious and cultural practices of other countries and financially supporting missionaries at home and abroad.[6]

§§§

In 1919, as the women's missionary work continued, Presbyterian minister, the Reverend V. Van Arsdale Nicholas and his wife Margaret, arrived to take over the pastorate at the church as part of the normal transition of leadership. In the early days, the focus of missionary work was evangelism to spread the word about Christianity and to effect conversions. After World War I, this was not so simple. The church was theologically split between the Fundamentalists upholding their view as the "true religion" and the Modernists who adopted a social gospel and creed that focused on dealing with practical

FIGURES 5-6.
A missionary collaboration:
Rev. V. Van Arsdale Nicholas,
c 1930s, and Grace A. Dow,
c mid-1920s, Herbert H. and
Grace A. Dow Family Papers,
Courtesy of The Herbert H. and
Grace A. Dow Foundation.

matters including improving the lives of individuals and addressing the social needs of the larger society.[7]

As these differing views were debated, Rev. Nicholas wanted to expand the missionary reach of the local Midland church[8] and the means was soon at hand. In 1925, the President of the Silliman Institute on the Island of Negros in the Philippines, Dr. David Sutherland Hibbard, came to the First Presbyterian Church in Midland and asked for help. In response, Rev. Nicholas told the congregation that he wanted the church to be in mission twenty-four hours a day, "with a missionary at work while the rest of the congregation took its nightly rest."[9]   Grace A. Dow stepped forward to do what she could by donating $1,100 that first year (about $13,500 in today's money) to partially fund the salary of a missionary to the Philippines.[10]   The chosen recipient was Metta Jacobs Archer, a widow in her thirties who had been sent by the national Presbyterian Church the previous year to teach English at Silliman Institute. [11]

Metta Jacobs Archer, the daughter of a Presbyterian pastor, Charles D. Jacobs, was born on October 17, 1891 in Ishpeming, Michigan near Marquette. Her mother, Abbie, died when she was twelve and her father remarried four years later. Her parents were tremendous supporters of missionary work and Metta wanted to take up that work even as a young child. She attended Eastern High School in Detroit, Michigan, graduating in June 1908, and then attended Western College (now Miami University) in Oxford, Ohio. In 1912, she began working as a Latin and English teacher at the high school in Marshall, Illinois. On July 6, 1915, she married Edward Ward Archer but he died four years later after a long illness. Metta's commitment to his care during the illness re-consecrated her religious faith. After additional teaching experience and receiving a master's degree in education from the University of Illinois in 1923, Metta received a call while in prayer to fill an urgent need for teachers at Silliman Institute. The Presbyterian Board of Foreign Missions accepted her application, and she sailed for the Philippines on May 8, 1924.[12]

Figure 7. Metta Jacobs Archer, c 1923, Record Group 360,
Courtesy of The Presbyterian Historical Society, Philadelphia, PA.

§§§

Upon her arrival, she discovered a well-established small college, Silliman Institute. The Institute had been founded on August 28, 1901, funded by an initial $10,000 gift to the Presbyterian Board that Dr. Horace Brinsmade Silliman of Cohoes, NY[13] made right after the Treaty of Paris was signed in 1898. The Treaty had ended the Spanish-American War, and Spain ceded the Philippines to the United States.[14] The express purpose of the gift was to set up an industrial school for boys in the Philippines—half a world away from the donor.[15] After exploration, the missionary in charge, Dr. David Hibbard,[16] selected a site on the southeast side of the Island of Negros in the city of Dumaguete.[17] The choice was based on the beauty of the city, the friendliness of the people, and the encouragement of both the Governor of Negros, Don Meliton Larena, and Rev. Captain John Anthony Randolph, the Chaplain of the 6th United States Infantry Regiment assigned to the island.[18]

The school started with fifteen young boys aged 12 to 16 years, but expanded rapidly; by the end of January 1902, enrollment had reached 114 students.[19] The student body grew from 226 to 882 students between 1905 and 1921 with the curricula covering third grade through high school and two years of college.[20] As the number of students and the school buildings grew over the years, Dr. Hibbard and the faculty gradually adjusted their curriculum towards the college level for older students.[21]

Silliman Institute was a typical college with the usual educational, social, and athletic activities, but a Christian religious atmosphere permeated school life, providing many opportunities for prayer groups, church services, and religious instruction that were part of extracurricular activities.[22] Parents of many faiths or no religious faith whatsoever sent their children there because Silliman Institute had a reputation for character building.[23] Although Sunday worship was expected of every student, there was no compulsion to accept evangelical Christianity— "only a loving tender invitation."[24] In addition, the focus from the beginning was to teach values relating to democratic thought with the goal of educating the students for liberty and self-government.[25]

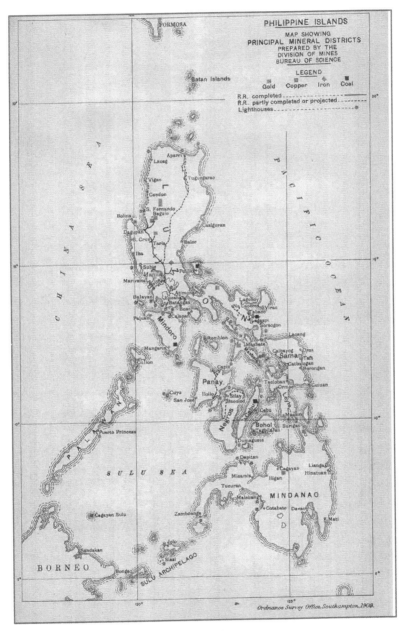

FIGURE 8.
The Philippine Islands, 1909. Note the Island of Negros near the center.
Ordnance Survey Office, Division of Mines, Southampton, England, Courtesy
of The Perry-Castañeda Library Map Collection, University of Texas at Austin.

FIGURE 9.
Travel map of the Island of Negros sent to Grace Dow, c 1940, Herbert H. and
Grace A. Dow Family Papers, Courtesy of the ExxonMobil and Courtesy of The
Herbert H. and Grace A. Dow Foundation.

A year after Metta Jacobs Archer arrived, Robert Silliman (only distantly related to the founder of the Institute) came to Silliman Institute.[26] Born on May 23, 1902, in Ravenswood, West Virginia, the son of Robert H. Silliman and Sophia Coleman, he graduated from Ravenswood High School in 1921, attended Marietta College in Marietta, Ohio for two years, and then went to the University of Chicago where he graduated in 1925. He briefly worked for the Swift meat packing company in Chicago and then accepted a temporary teaching position in the history department at Silliman Institute on May 17, 1926. He met Metta at the college and they married on March 18, 1927 on the adjacent island of Cebu. The service was performed by Dr. Dunlap, a Presbyterian Minister who had spoken at Metta's father's church in Ottumwa, Iowa years earlier.[27]

FIGURE 10.
Robert Silliman graduation photograph, c 1925, Record Group 360, Courtesy of The Presbyterian Historical Society, Philadelphia, PA.

§§§

After Metta's marriage to Robert, Grace Dow continued to fund a portion of the couple's salary and later pensions for their lifetimes.[28] Grace was already actively involved in local civic, club, and church activities, but above all, she was known for her quiet acts of charity and deep faith. With no fanfare, she would tend to the needs of others, provide a casserole for a family suffering illness, and supply a used violin, clothing, or a toy as needed. Though the extent of her support for the Sillimans was not fully known to members of her own church congregation for many years,[29] she took on this commitment because the tenets of the Presbyterian Church include that "man has the responsibility of ministering to others that cannot be left up to the clergy alone."[30] Grace was a Christian and believed the doctrine of "man's unselfish and sacrificial service."[31] Within the Presbyterian Church this also meant using the gifts you were given for the common good of society.[32]

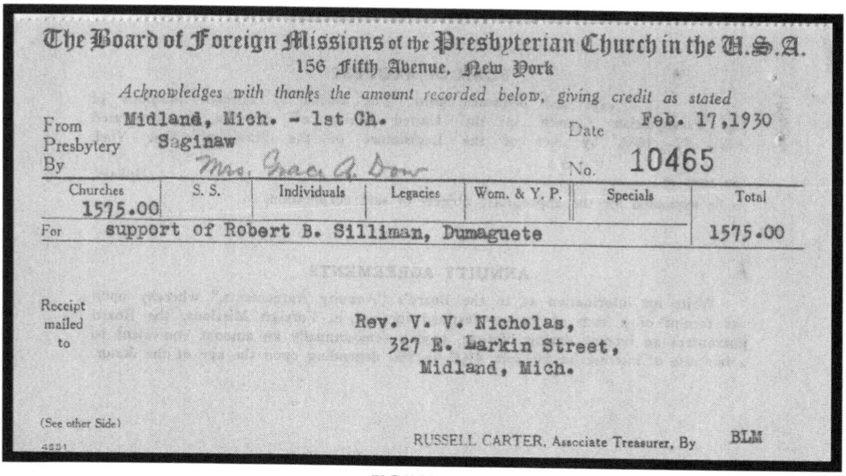

The Board of Foreign Missions of the Presbyterian Church in the U.S.A.
156 Fifth Avenue, New York

Acknowledges with thanks the amount recorded below, giving credit as stated

From	Midland, Mich. - 1st Ch.					Date	Feb. 17, 1930	
Presbytery	Saginaw							
By	Mrs. Grace A. Dow					No.	10465	
Churches	S. S.	Individuals	Legacies	Wom. & Y. P.		Specials		Total
1575.00								
For	support of Robert B. Silliman, Dumaguete							1575.00

Receipt mailed to

Rev. V. V. Nicholas,
327 E. Larkin Street,
Midland, Mich.

(See other Side)

RUSSELL CARTER, Associate Treasurer, By   BLM

FIGURE 11.
Receipt for donation for a portion of the Sillimans' salaries, 1930, Courtesy of The Memorial Presbyterian Church Archives, Midland, MI.

Her support is apparent now, not only because the church kept good financial records, but also because the Sillimans wrote almost weekly letters to their patron, Grace Dow.[33] The result is an incredibly personal record of their triumphs, their pain, their travels, their fears, their efforts to teach, their faith, and their missionary work at the college and among the mountain tribes people.[34]

Not all the correspondence survives, of course. The first extant letter between Grace Dow and the Sillimans dates from 1931. But it is clear from even the earliest correspondence that they had already established a close collaborative relationship. The Sillimans had shared photos, postcards, and information earlier about the Silliman Institute so Grace knew about their surroundings and their activities and those of their missionary colleagues.

FIGURE 12.
First location for Silliman Institute, 1923. One of the many postcard images sent by the Sillimans to Grace Dow. Herbert H. and Grace A. Dow Family Papers, Courtesy of The Herbert H. and Grace A. Dow Foundation.

FIGURE 13.
Silliman Bible School (Channon Hall), 1924, Herbert H. and Grace A. Dow Family
Papers, Courtesy of The Herbert H. and Grace A. Dow Foundation.

FIGURE 14.
Mission Hospital (Katipun Gathering Hall), c 1920s, sent to Grace Dow by the
Sillimans; Herbert H. and Grace A. Dow Family Papers, Courtesy of The Herbert H.
and Grace A. Dow Foundation.

FIGURE 15.
Domestic Science Class, c 1920s, Herbert H. and Grace A. Dow Family Papers,
Courtesy of The Herbert H. and Grace A. Dow Foundation.

FIGURE 16.
Vacation Bible School, 1927, Herbert H. and Grace A. Dow Family Papers, Courtesy
of The Herbert H. and Grace A. Dow Foundation.

The work in Dumaguete was multifaceted. The Sillimans were both teachers, Metta in English[35] and Bob in history, but their involvement with the college, the students, and the community was much more than this. As was typical with foreign missionaries "on station" within a college setting, they had many roles, including serving on faculty committees, leading prayer groups and Bible classes, working as club advisors, and maintaining social contacts with the students and community members by providing frequent Sunday dinners.[36] The Sillimans were interested in the physical, educational, and spiritual welfare of their students.[37] Trying to find financial support for students to keep them at the college was also a challenge. In a sense, their missionary work was not so much preaching their faith as much as living it, being good stewards, and providing witness to their beliefs in how they treated others. [38]

Their bond with Grace Dow—a collaborative relationship which would last for almost four decades—was created through their faith and through sharing letters. Professing her faith as she went through some

FIGURE 17.
Metta Silliman, c 1930s, Record Group 360, Courtesy of The Presbyterian Historical
Society, Philadelphia, PA.

difficult times after the death of Herbert Dow, Grace Dow wrote the Sillimans, "I know I have the dear Lord Jesus Christ...to cling to."[39] The Sillimans felt strongly that they, too, were in the Philippines because of their faith and their calling to that field of service. Bob said,

> That is why He sent us here and why He gave us to you and you to us. No people in the world at the present time need Him more than the young people and the leaders of this nation. Their world future and destiny depends upon their trusting Him and their following and building their nation upon His way of life.[40]

§§§

As a worldwide depression took hold in the 1930s, the Sillimans, like others, sacrificed with cuts in their salaries from the Presbyterian Church Board as overall resources were reduced. As a result, in addition to providing a portion of their salaries, Grace Dow began to send gifts of clothing and other goods, whatever was necessary, thousands of miles by boat to supplement their needs.[41] She also sent them quarterly and sometimes monthly checks of $50 or $100 (worth about $1,660 in today's money),[42] a separate one to each to use for their own needs or to distribute as needed to others.[43] This gave them tremendous flexibility to help others when someone needed financial assistance. It may have meant distributing eggs and milk to students with tuberculosis, buying someone a new pair of shoes or a dress, or contributing to some of their students' tuition or room and board costs.[44]

In addition to facilitating their missionary work, the monetary gifts from Grace Dow also provided the Sillimans with creature comforts that helped offset the distance from home and the hardships of the tropics. They had a very comfortable house in town, and like many of the Silliman professors and the more prosperous Filipino families in Dumaguete, a mountain cottage retreat (called "Fern Rest") at Camp Lookout about ten miles

FIGURES 18-19.
The Silliman's Dumaguete home: exterior porch facing Langheim Road and interior, c 1930s, Herbert H. and Grace A. Dow Family Papers, Courtesy The Herbert H. and Grace A. Dow Foundation.

outside of town. The retreat, which they used on weekends and holidays to escape the heat in the lowlands, put them in direct contact with the approximately 150 Filipino families living along the adjacent mountain

FIGURE 20.
The Silliman's mountain retreat, "Fern Rest" at Camp Lookout, c 1930s, Herbert H. and Grace A. Dow Family Papers, Courtesy of The Herbert H. and Grace A. Dow Foundation.

ridge from whom they bought eggs, fruit, and vegetables.[45]   These interactions significantly broadened their missionary outreach.

Christmas became a major time to distribute gifts of clothing, cakes of Ivory hand soap, dolls, small toys, pencils, and bags of candy and peanuts to their mountain neighbors. [46] At Christmas in 1936, their generosity having become known, they were overwhelmed when fifty mountain people showed up unexpectedly at their mountain camp to receive presents.[47] Metta and her younger sister, Abby R. Jacobs,[48] who had come to live in Dumaguete in 1931 and was also supported by Grace Dow, scrambled to find and distribute gifts from what they had on hand, even delving into their own meager stores and clothing at the cottage to find suitable presents. Realizing then they needed to plan ahead for Christmas 1937, Metta commented to a family member,

Next year, we shall be prepared for the crowd, for we intend to begin at once laying aside a few centavos each month for the purpose. A cake or two of soap put aside occasionally, a towel, or washcloth and by next December we shall have a supply on hand. Their joy and happiness over these gifts makes one wish he might do much more.[49]

Help was on its way. Up to this point, Grace Dow had provided a significant part of the Sillimans' financial support for their work without assistance from her church congregation. Soon after the arrival of the new pastor, the Reverend John Gardner, in 1937, church-wide support for this project was brought under the auspices of the women of the Missionary Society.[50] According to Bob Silliman this marked the beginning of the First Presbyterian Church of Midland's annual donations of material to fill the boxes and trunks with gifts for the Christmas distribution.[51]

FIGURE 21.
Rev. John Gardner, c 1930s, Courtesy of The Memorial Presbyterian Church
Archives, Midland, MI.

FIGURES 22-23.
Mountain villager, Simiona, top, second from left, her family, and below other villagers gather for Christmas distributions, 1940, Herbert H. and Grace A. Dow Family Papers, Courtesy of The Herbert H. and Grace A. Dow Foundation.

The first of the church boxes are not well documented, but for the Christmas of 1939, Bob Silliman comments that between the box from "the Midland folks," and the supplemental money from Grace Dow for soap, candy, and toys, twenty-eight neighboring mountain families including 198 people received gifts. Every person received an article of clothing (a dress, shirt, sweater, etc.) and a toy or candy. Every family also received soap. The families attended the Christmas service in their language spoken by a Filipino pastor brought in especially for the purpose.[52]

§§§

The supplemental funds also allowed the Sillimans to travel within the country to see the sites and visit missions of other church groups. The Philippines has a rich cultural heritage with 65 minority groups that speak over 87 different languages. In 1934, among their trips, the Sillimans took a six-day trip to the northern part of the island of Luzon, north of

FIGURE 24.
An Igorot payag, a traditional elevated Filipino hut, 1930s, Herbert H. and Grace A. Dow Family Papers, Courtesy of The Herbert H. and Grace A. Dow Foundation.

Negros.[53] The Sillimans visited native tribal people called the Igorot, who lived in the mountain areas of Luzon. These people were

indigenous to Luzon before the Spanish, and then the Americans, colo-
nized the Philippines. They still lived in primitive conditions in 1934.
Occasionally a child from this region, usually one who was Christianized,
would find his or her way down to Silliman Institute in Dumaguete.[54]

FIGURE 25.
Igorot people visited by the Sillimans in northern Luzon, 1934, Herbert H. and Grace
A. Dow Family Papers, Courtesy of The Herbert H. and Grace A. Dow Foundation.

§§§

Despite the occasional trip exploring the country, the Sillimans' main
focus was their educational and missionary work. Professions of faith
were part of life at Silliman Institute, and special encouragement of
such was provided around Founders Day each year in the fall (modeled,
according to documents from the time, on the American Fourth of July
mid-western small town spirit). Celebrations were held with parades,
prayer meetings of thanksgiving, lectures from visiting alumni, athletic
events, and special meals for the whole community. A few weeks later,
Decision Day was celebrated. On this occasion, leading college students would speak about their decision to accept Christianity.

FIGURE 26.
Founders Day Parade, 1933, Herbert H. and Grace A. Dow Family Papers, Courtesy
of The Herbert H. and Grace A. Dow Foundation.

During Decision Day in 1938, the year Silliman became a University,[55] a student gave the following profession of faith,

> As I grew up I began to doubt the religion in which I had been brought up. My grandmother thought me irreligious…but I wasn't irreligious. I wanted to know the truth about the great Creator of heaven and earth. I wanted a God to worship, a God that existed, a God that loves and guides. Hence it was that I came to Silliman. My grandmother had tried to help me out. However, she knew nothing of the Bible or the answers for my questioning mind. When I came to Silliman, I noticed a good deal of difference in the attitude of the people here. Why I asked myself, are they different from the people I know? I have seen those who have professed Christ here, their faces gleaming with a new life and hope, some with tears in their eyes. I saw another group this morning; yes,

> I saw them, for I was one of them. I stood this morning because I was desperately in need of a real companion, a real Lord and Savior...I am standing here tonight to witness for Him. I have found the God I was seeking, a God of worship, an understanding God...the Savior who gave His life for me that I may be redeemed from sin.[56]

This profession of faith was one of several examples reported by Robert Silliman in the *Quarterly Newsletter* from Dumaguete Station sent to Midland for Grace Dow and the women of the First Presbyterian Church Missionary Society.

§§§

The Sillimans were back in the United States in 1937 for a long furlough while Bob finished his Master's Degree at Lafayette College in Pennsylvania.[57] During that time Metta came to Midland to share news of their work in the Philippines with the First Presbyterian Church Missionary Society.[58] But world events would soon test the work and faith of the Sillimans and many others.

Throughout the 1930s there had been growing concern in the Philippines about Japan's incursions into China. The two countries had fought intermittently since 1931, but in July 7, 1937, a full-scale Second Sino-Japanese War broke out. Japan had imperialist sights on China and its natural resources that clashed with China's rising nationalism.[59] In letters from the Philippines to Grace Dow, the Sillimans said, "If Japan takes the Dutch East Indies [Indonesia], how long will it be before she enters the war and sets her eyes on the Philippines in spite of the USA?"[60] On the other side of the world, German Chancellor Adolf Hitler's invasions in Poland, Holland, the Netherlands, and France from September 1939 to May 1940 were also alarming.[61]

An American destroyer appeared in Dumaguete harbor in August 1940, the first boat of its kind to come to the area in many years, and the community wondered about its presence. The purpose of the visit was secret but Metta felt that, "the officers were checking the number of Americans in town, the availability of radio communications, and how many grocery and medical supplies were in stock."[62]

The destroyer's visit in August had already raised everyone's anxiety level so when the German-Italian-Japanese Tripartite Pact, allying the three country's military aims, was announced on the radio in September 1940, the Sillimans felt it might be only a matter of hours before the United States and Japan would be at war. Rumors abounded about U. S. warships on the way to Manila from Hawaii, and many saw the situation as serious, creating a state of hysteria in the Philippines. Bob Silliman commented to Grace Dow, "Should the U. S. get into the war we would be trapped like rats." Bob and Metta agreed to start buying a supply of canned goods and store them at the mountain cabin, and Bob even purchased a 22-caliber rifle and some ammunition for defense. He commented further,

> The one thing I know is that Japanese soldiers will never take my wife or myself alive. I know this is a great way for a missionary to talk but this is an example of what war and the fear of war does to people. We have heard too many tales of eyewitnesses from China of what the Japanese have done there.[63]

Most of the merchants in Dumaguete were Chinese and they had been actively sending money to China to help out in the war, so when in February 1941, the central business district of the town was destroyed by fire, there was some concern that it was a case of sabotage.[64] Besides the fact that the town had no fire-fighting equipment or a single trained firefighter, buildings were built very close together in Dumaguete and their roofs were made of flammable woven nipa palms making it virtually impossible to stop a fire. Although Silliman University was untouched, eight commercial blocks of the city burned and one thousand people lost their homes.

The town looked to Silliman University for protection and the college extended their mission again to meet the need. Bob Silliman helped coordinate the relief efforts to bring in food and prevent profiteering.[65] Metta recounted her fears to Grace Dow, commenting,

> The horror of the fire made me dread the nights, and for several weeks I couldn't sleep without waking suddenly during the night and imagining I smelled smoke. Even now every night I put a chair beside my bed and on it my kimono, slippers, and flashlight. Foolish, isn't it? Yes, and whenever our bell rings, I listen alertly and count the strokes to see whether it is announcing the time or a fire....We all feel as though we're sitting on top of a seething volcano which may erupt at any moment. Our main job is to keep calm, to keep our friends calm, and to go on from day to day. Surely, we must keep our nerves steady, but it is hard sometimes not to get a bit jittery.[66]

FIGURE 27.
The Japanese were warned about their incursions in East Asia in a newspaper article from February 1941, sent to Grace Dow by the Sillimans from the Philippines, Herbert H. and Grace A. Dow Family Papers, Courtesy of The Herbert H. and Grace A. Dow Foundation and Rights Reserved Courtesy of *The Manila Bulletin Publishing Corporation*, Manila, Philippines.

The fire was another warning sign of things to come, and in March, Bob Silliman became part of a preparedness committee that surveyed foodstuffs, arranged for medical care, set up plans to investigate possible espionage, and even created evacuation plans in case the Japanese invaded.[67] This was still eight months before the Japanese attacked Pearl Harbor in Hawaii. Although some Americans may have professed surprise at the attack, correspondence from the Sillimans in East Asia to Grace Dow and their friends at the First Presbyterian Church shows that many people had long been well aware and highly concerned about the danger posed by the Japanese.[68] Grace invited the Sillimans to come stay with her "awhile" should they be forced home by Japanese activities.[69]

§§§

Despite their worry about Japanese activities in East Asia, the Sillimans continued their work. Bob worked with the head American missionary nurse at the hospital at Silliman University to plan and build a clinic and combined community house for the mountain people they served. Grace Dow provided some of the funds for this building and Bob commented:

> Should we give the place a nice name it should be called the Dow Hospital or at least the Midland clinic. As usual we get most of the credit when it is your money and not ours that have made this possible. Anyway in the name of our Filipino mountain friends I wish to again thank you for having made the little project possible.[70]

The building also provided a place for daily vacation Bible school for small children and adults, and Bob told Grace Dow, "There is really no end to the opportunities for Christian service in the Philippines, religious, educational, or medical."[71]

FIGURES 28-29.
Clinic and Community House the Sillimans had built for their mountain friends, 1941;
Metta and her sister Abby painting the clinic's furnishings, Herbert H. and Grace A.
Dow Family Papers, Courtesy of The Herbert H. and Grace A. Dow Foundation.

§§§

Back in Dumaguete, as a precautionary measure, all Americans were asked to register with the Red Cross, and the American Silliman faculty was surveyed to determine if they could pay their own way home if evacuated.[72] A trip by the Sillimans to Manila in June 1941 for medical care revealed streets full of American soldiers, and American ships, planes, and submarines were everywhere.[73] With radio news at the end of July 1941 that President Franklin D. Roosevelt had frozen Japanese assets in the U. S., virtually embargoing Japanese exports and imports, they awaited Japan's next move and shared their worries with Grace Dow, saying, "Anything can happen."[74] The Sillimans continued to put away food supplies in Dumaguete and at the mountain camp house, and they planned to plant corn, beans, and other vegetables in the camp garden in case the boat service that brought them fresh food supplies was suspended. They even experimented with a substitute for potatoes and rice in case they became unavailable: coarsely ground corn meal made into mush and sliced and fried.[75]

Metta soon commented that mail was becoming erratic,[76] and her response to a mid-October 1941 birthday card from Mrs. Dorothy Wilson and thirty-two members of the First Presbyterian Church Missionary Society was the last communication Midlanders received for quite a while.[77]

Two months later, the Japanese bombed Pearl Harbor. The Sillimans heard the announcement on the radio, and they flipped from channel to channel hoping for more news. As various channels repeated the words, "Bombs fell on Oahu," "Bombs fell on Oahu," Bob Silliman commented to Metta and her sister Abby, "Which means, gals, that we're in for it."[78]

Manila was bombed from the air on December 9th and days later the Philippines was invaded. Panicked parents quickly called Silliman University students home; by mid-December the only students left on campus were those whose home areas such as Luzon and Davao were already involved in the fighting, making their return home

impossible.[79]   On January 3, 1942, six hundred Silliman University
ROTC students were called into the new United States Army Forces Far
East (U.S.A.F.F.E.) under General Douglas MacArthur.   After receiving
rigorous training, they moved to northern parts of Negros to face the
expected enemy invasion.[80]   There had been hope initially that the U.S.
and Filipino troops would be able to contain the enemy but the Filipino
islands fell one by one from the enemy's pounding air raids and sheer
superiority in numbers.[81]

FIGURE 30.
Japanese bomb Manila, Philippines, December 1941, Courtesy of The National
Archives and Records Administration.

As the Americans in Dumaguete waited for the Japanese to arrive,
blackout precautions–difficult with the open lattice upper walls used
for ventilation in Filipino homes–were taken.   Many Sillimanarians
stepped up to help with preparations.   University records, food supplies,

FIGURE 31.
Surrender of American troops on Corregidor, May 1942, re-staged for the
cameras, 208-AA-80B-1, Courtesy of The National Archives and Records
Administration.

bookstore texts, science equipment, and some library books were scattered at various points away from the coast or stored in an underground vault in the partially finished church building. Private possessions were buried.[82] The University Press that Bob Silliman had, in an extra-curricular capacity, shepherded for several years, printing notices, pamphlets, letterhead, and the weekly university newspaper, now became a fulltime job for both him and Abby Jacobs. They continued to print the

Sillimanarian newspaper until April 10, 1942 to keep the community informed and reduce rumors. The American Army also began using the *Sillimanarian's* linotype machine to print forms and emergency money.[83]

§§§

When Bataan and Corregidor fell on May 6, it was clear that Japanese troops would fan out to the rest of the Philippine islands. A Japanese warship finally arrived on the Island of Negros on May 26, 1942, and a transport landed forty Japanese soldiers and their commander, Capt. H. J. Tsuda, in Dumaguete.[84] They found the campus deserted. Beginning months earlier, the American teachers and seventy-five Filipino faculty members had fled to the hills in the southern part of the island.[85] They had decided to separate into small groups, figuring it would be harder for the Japanese to capture them if they were scattered.[86] Several families had left in January and fled west to Malabo, a farming village of almost 300 people[87] which eventually became the home of the free government.[88] In April, the Sillimans and Abby Jacobs went to an area about 15 kilometers west of Dumaguete. But on May 4, 1942, a few weeks before the Japanese landed, they fled farther south to the village of Casala-an in the foothills of the Siaton area fifty kilometers southwest of Dumaguete because it was comparatively desolate country at the time with thick forests and clusters of hills with only scarce amounts of corn, rice, or cattle that might induce the Japanese troops to forage for food.[89] In addition, the Sillimans' household helpers, Gliceria and Dinsay, had grown up in that area, knew the people and customs, and could "vouch" for the Americans.[90]

Their first home in hiding, built on a farm owned by their housemaid's brother, was a typical rural bamboo *payag* much like they had seen on their visit to the Igorots in the 1930s. It was built of strips of rattan with a roof of dried nipa palm fronds and raised off the ground about five feet to keep out snakes and mud.[91] Only two days after the Japanese landed in Dumaguete, a truckload of soldiers arrived in the Siaton area

FIGURE 32.
Hills and Forests around Casala-an in the Siaton area where the Silliman's hid in
1942-1944. Photo 2008, Courtesy of Frederick S. Dael.

asking for the Sillimans. The Japanese troops had a complete list of all
the Americans and their evacuation plans, obtained from a Filipino col-
laborator. Fortunately, a runner from the village alerted the Americans
to the soldiers' arrival, and the remoteness of their hideout gave them
enough time to escape.

After that scare, the Sillimans moved constantly and managed to
stay one step ahead of the Japanese. Eventually they moved among
seven different payags prepared and supplied ahead of time and hidden even farther in the jungle. As they fled from place to place,
their Filipino friends, friends of friends, and the Filipino guerrillas
fighting the Japanese protected them.[92] They came perilously close
to capture a few times, and as they hid, they even heard the Japanese
soldiers calling their names and coaxing them to surrender saying,
"Mr. Seeleeman! Mr. Seeleeman! Be kind to us. Come down to us.
Do not be foolish."[93]

§§§

For the Sillimans' family and extended family it must have seemed as if they had fallen off the edge of the earth. The Red Cross had not listed them as being in a concentration camp, so their family thought they were dead. Unbeknownst to Bob, his mother even wrote to Mrs. Douglas MacArthur, wife of the U. S. general serving as Field Marshall of the Philippine Army during this time to see if her husband could determine their whereabouts.[94] The Sillimans were eventually listed incorrectly as "prisoners of war" with the Office of the Provost Marshal General of the Army since there had been no contact with them outside the Island of Negros for some time.[95]

It was a difficult two years for Bob, Metta, and Abby with meager rations of corn, bananas, coconuts, sweet potatoes, wild native tomatoes, and occasionally fish or meat brought by the guerrilla fighters. Living conditions were primitive and they had no access to medical care. Their clothes and shoes were in tatters.[96] They suffered mind-numbing boredom from lack of contact with other people and lack of access to reading material or news but kept themselves busy with the unending work required of subsistence living: chopping wood, grinding corn on a stone, cooking over an open fire, washing their clothes in mountain streams, fetching water, and later helping care for baby Eleanor who was born to two of their companions in hiding, former students Joaquin and Nui Funda.[97]

However, by early 1943, Bob was asked by guerrilla leader Jesus Villamor, a pilot and war hero and son of the former President of the University of Philippines, to help with the guerrilla movement. Villamor was responsible for coordinating the activities of rival guerrilla bands. Some were seeking power while others— upland farmers or Silliman University faculty and students —had been spurred to join the guerrilla war by the brutality of the Japanese. There was also a sizable group of Silliman University ROTC students who had not surrendered to the enemy.[98] Bob's mere presence in the area inspired the fighters as he became involved as an agent gathering intelligence to pass onto the Filipino Army.[99]

The free civil government had been established by Silliman University Professor Roy Bell in the hills of Malabo west of Dumaguete. After a few months of guerrilla work, Bob left Metta and Abby behind hiding north of the Siaton area and moved to Malabo when, on June 12, 1943, Governor Alfredo Montelibano appointed him Deputy Governor for the southern Negros Oriental,[100] the only non-Filipino so honored.[101] Six days later, invading Japanese troops destroyed the free government capital, forcing its move to the village of Casala-an in the Siaton area where the Silliman family was still in hiding. Governmental records were also concealed here and survived the war intact.[102]

Bob Silliman worked to reorganize the municipal governments and to secure foodstuffs to feed guerrilla units and civilian populations in the free territories, acted as a go-between for governmental couriers, and arranged for payment of guerrilla troops with newly printed emergency pesos.[103]

One of Bob's students wrote after the war, the guerrillas worked hand-in-hand with the Filipino and American Armies and there was "…a special relationship—warm as blood ties—between Filipinos and Americans, who, at some glorious point in time…, braved the same hardships together as members of one family." [104] Fifteen hundred freedom-fighters sacrificed their lives on Negros to keep a portion of the island in free territory.

Bob was often separated from Metta and Abby and wouldn't see them for weeks at time as he worked for the government in town and they stayed hidden in the hills.[105] They all lived in constant fear of capture that had to have repeatedly tested their nerves, their patience, their resolve, and their faith.

§§§

Finally, on November 23, 1943, the Sillimans received a message from guerrilla Col. Salvador Abcede, via Roy Bell, that a submarine was expected in Negros waters soon to evacuate the American Silliman University faculty and other Americans interested in being repatriated to the United States.[106] At that time, few American families from the Silliman University faculty remained free. They moved again and again farther up the mountains as the Japanese tightened their search and they narrowly escaped several more times.[107] Of the twenty-one American faculty members at Silliman, only ten escaped eventual capture by the Japanese. Those captured were taken to Manila and interned.[108] Unfortunately, several families had been captured only days before potential rescue.[109] The Americans fully expected to be tortured and executed if caught, as the Japanese had done to their missionary and university colleagues on other islands in the Philippines.[110] In fact, the Japanese ordered the execution of all Americans caught after January 1, 1944.[111]

The first rendezvous with the submarine was scheduled for December 4; none of the Americans were able to make it, each having to escape unexpected Japanese patrols.[112] Fortunately, they had a second opportunity for rescue. On January 29, 1944, they began a fifty kilometers (thirty-one miles) hike, some of it at night, around the southern tip of the island and headed northwest along the ocean to reach the village of Basay.[113] Various American missionaries and their families were asked to converge in the area and wait for their deliverance. On February 7, 1944, the Sillimans, Abby Jacobs, and other evacuees escaped by boarding sailboats and waiting for the U.S.S. Narwhal to surface offshore. The U.S.S. Narwhal, a huge cruiser submarine with the largest submarine deck guns in the United States Navy, had been designed to hunt and sink enemy vessels. The Narwhal's distinguished service during World War II included conducting fifteen patrols, sinking eight enemy ships, landing allied agents in hostile territory, rescuing numerous civilians such as the group from Negros, and transporting supplies to the allies within enemy territory.[114] This rescue mission included U. S. Army personnel who had been ordered to Australia, the Sillimans and Abby Jacobs, and more than twenty other Americans who had also been in hiding. Among them were Silliman University President Arthur Carson, his wife Edith, and their children, Roy and Edna Mae Bell and their children, Mildred and Anna Edwards, and the McKinley family.[115]

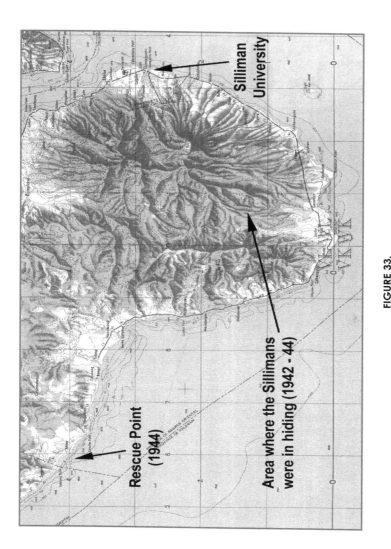

FIGURE 33.
Map of the southern portion of the Island of Negros, showing the difficult terrain offering some measure of protection from the Japanese. Annotations indicate the location of Silliman University in Dumaguete, the Silliman's approximate hiding location in Casala-an in the Siaton area during 1942-1944, and their rescue point off Basay in 1944. Army Map Service 1955 (NC 51-10), Courtesy of The Perry-Castañeda Library Map Collection, University of Texas at Austin; Annotations by Robert G. Nelb.

FIGURE 34.
U. S. S. Narwhal (SS-167) Submarine sitting at the dock at the Mars Island Navy Yard, Vallejo, CA, north of San Francisco, March 28, 1943 a year before it was used to evacuate the Sillimans to Australia. Photo 19-N-42920, Courtesy of The U. S. Navy History and Heritage Command and the National Archives and Records Administration.

After it rescued the Americans that night, the submarine crew off-loaded 45 tons of cargo including 1,500 carbines, 10 cases of machine guns, Browning automatics, 375,000 rounds of ammunition, medical and other needed supplies for the guerrilla fighters by transferring the supplies to 25 small sailboats that came alongside before the sub sped away from the island.[116]

During the eight day trip to Darwin, Australia, the Americans were treated to wonderful food, most of which they had not seen in more than two years. Upon arrival, the Red Cross located them in the seaside resort of Caloundra, north of Brisbane, for recuperation. While there, the Silliman faculty met with General MacArthur who asked them, "How does it feel to be raised from the dead?"[117]

§§§

The Sillimans returned to the United States by hospital ship on May 2, 1944.[118] They had hoped to be assigned to Midland, Michigan immediately but their precarious health from two years in hiding made that impossible. The Presbyterian Board doctor put his foot down and required them to rest and receive treatment for starvation and a galaxy of internal parasites such as hookworms and various amoebae they had picked up from their poor living conditions while in hiding. Metta was also in pain from a broken coccyx (tailbone) she had suffered in a fall during one of their frequent flights from the Japanese.[119] Bob was able to come to Midland and stay with Grace Dow in the summer of 1944 and Metta followed in September.[120] Their time in hiding had been traumatic, but after a while Metta was happy to report that her dreams and nightmares of being pursued by the Japanese were occurring less frequently, and they were both thrilled to hear of the bombing of Japanese targets in Dumaguete by American forces in September 1944.[121]

They began to set up a promotional office for Silliman University in New York and started collecting books and materials for their eventual return to Dumaguete.[122] The majority of the 45,000 books in the university library had been destroyed in the Japanese soldiers' attempt to wipe out all traces of Western Culture.[123]   Rev. John Gardner of the Midland First Presbyterian Church suggested an idea to rebuild the Silliman library holdings. The committee set up to facilitate this, chaired by Mrs. S. L. Starks, would serve as a model for other churches also gathering books for the project throughout the United States.[124] The Midland church sent literally a ton of books to Silliman University to help restock the library.[125]

On October 20, 1944, several weeks after the first American bombing in the Philippines, General MacArthur returned to the Philippines. Sillimanians in the U.S. eagerly awaited the recapture of Manila so they could hear the fate of the thirty-five Presbyterian missionaries from all over the Philippines who were interned there.[126]

FIGURE 35.
General Douglas MacArthur wades ashore at Leyte, Philippines, October 1944, Photo 111-SC-407101, Courtesy of The National Archives and Records Administration.

The Sillimans had high expectations to return to the Philippines where they felt they had a clear calling.[127] While they waited and planned the work for their return, they traveled around the United States to share their missionary story with other churches.[128] They visited Midland again in March 1945 to take part in Lenten activities and to tell their story.[129] They were actually limited on what they could say in their presentation. The war was still being waged on Negros Island and they feared a few Japanese puppet rulers might cause harm to the Filipino Silliman faculty and friends. They couldn't mention where they left the island and could not discuss specific names of guerrillas on Negros.[130] They commented during their visit, "Filipinos sacrificed their lives to keep the American flag flying over Bataan and Corregidor. ...Is it a wonder that we want to return to these people just as soon as we can?"[131]

After their return to New York from Midland that spring, Grace Dow told them she would make provisions for their support after her death both with gifts of stock and cash.[132] This was a tremendous relief for the Sillimans and they were extremely touched by her commitment to them.

Sillimans To Resume Teaching Jobs At Presbyterian School In Philippines

By June Neeb

Mr. and Mrs. Robert Silliman leave Midland today to return as teachers at the Presbyterian-founded Silliman university in the Philippines. They will go back to the islands where they hid out in the hills from the Japanese for more than two years before they were able to escape to the United States in 1944.

The Sillimans have been visiting for four days at their "home church," the First Presbyterian church of Midland which sponsors their activities in the Philippines.

They plan to sail from New York City by freighter during the first week of June and make the trip to Manila, via the Panama Canal, in about 35 days. From Manila they will go by inter-island steamer about 420 miles south to Dumaguete on Negros Island, where the university is located.

The Sillimans were honored at a potluck supper at the church Sunday evening. Farewell gifts were presented to them jointly by the Women's Federation, the Women's Missionary society and the Session. Mrs. Silliman's gift was a plastic handbag, while Silliman received an authentic leather brief case.

While here Silliman was guest speaker at the weekly Kiwanis club.
See SILLIMANS—Page 4

Mr. and Mrs. Robert Silliman

FIGURE 36.
Silliman's visit Midland and plan to return to the Philippines in the summer of 1946. Article published May 7, 1946, Courtesy of The *Midland Daily News* and Tawny Ryan Nelb.

After another visit to Midland in May 1946, the Sillimans began preparations for their return to the Philippines. Dr. Arthur Carson and his wife Edith, who had escaped from Negros with the Sillimans on the U.S.S. Narwhal,[133] were the first missionary couple to return to the Philippines; the Sillimans, the second returning couple, followed in the summer of 1946. The Filipino faculty had reopened the university in July 1945 after the American army entered Dumaguete in April 26, 1945.

Most of the buildings survived, probably because they housed Japanese soldiers and were used to store the loot the soldiers had plundered from the island. But the campus was gutted of furniture and equipment, and every building needed repairs. Many building floors had been dug up to create defensive bunkers and air raid shelters for a last ditch death stand by the Japanese. Unfortunately, the president's home and the Conservatory of Music were destroyed by fire.[134]

By the time the Sillimans returned in August 1946, the campus was already alive with activity. Buildings were actively being cleaned and repaired[135] and over 2,500 students had enrolled—the school's largest enrollment ever. The Sillimans both started teaching again immediately.[136]

§§§

The First Presbyterian Church in Midland eventually sent boxes of goods to help fill the shortages of clothing and other necessities in Dumaguete. Dorothy Wilson, secretary of the church since 1939, facilitated this interaction from 1948-1954, putting together multiple packages worth less than $10 each so as not to violate customs regulations and incur tariff charges.[137] She sent over 106 packages which the Sillimans distributed to the people of Dumaguete and their long-time mountain friends on behalf of the Missionary Society.

Over the years, donations included yard goods and other sewing material that could be made into clothing by Metta, her house staff, and some of her students for distribution,[138] as well as toys, cosmetics, soap, and even powdered milk and vitamins.[139] The church continued sending boxes until 1965.[140]

FIGURE 37.
Memorial Presbyterian Church, 1953, Courtesy of The Memorial
Presbyterian Church Archives.

§§§

The Sillimans visited Midland on their infrequent furloughs and shared their experiences in the Philippines with the local church.[141] On one of those visits, on January 6, 1951, the Presbyterian Church in Midland received them into official membership.[142] The pastor, John Gardner commented to the congregation at the time, "In these days we are all aware of the importance of extending Christianity around the world. We do it through missionaries, and these two friends are our representatives."[143]

Bob Silliman was elected Vice President of Silliman University in 1952 but took on many additional duties when the new Filipino President, Leopoldo T. Ruiz, the former Philippine consul-general in Chicago, became ill.[144] Bob served as acting president from 1961-1962.[145]

FIGURE 38.
Silliman University Vice President
Robert Silliman, 1964, Courtesy
of Frederick S. Dael.

FIGURE 39.
Grace A. Dow, 1943, Herbert
H. and Grace A. Dow Family
Papers, Courtesy of The
Herbert H. and Grace A. Dow
Foundation.

The Sillimans were deeply saddened when their patron, Grace Dow, died in June 1953. They had called her "their guardian angel,"[146] and after her death the Sillimans told their "Midland Friends" that their lives and the fulfillment of their mission were a living monument to her.[147] She had provided for the Sillimans after her death with financial resources, but few realized how many other ways she had helped them financially previously and how in turn they had helped her. Grace Dow's gifts to the Sillimans had been gifts of altruism, a sense of responsibility to follow church tenets, and faith. But it is clear their relationship became so close over the years that they treated each other as family.[148] Bob commented at one point that he wrote to her "just as often and just like I write my own mother."[149] After Herbert H. Dow's death in 1930, and with her children out on their own, the Sillimans had given Grace Dow a substitute family to care for and to worry over. Truly, the Sillimans and their work had inspired Grace Dow to continue her mission of helping others.[150]

§§§

Over their remaining years of service in the Philippines, the Sillimans helped many children. Having no children of their own, they raised three older foster children whose parents were not deceased but needed additional financial help. These children became very special to them and were like their own. Emma Cole (now Teves), their first, was born in 1934. She eventually graduated from the Silliman School of Nursing and worked in the profession both in the Philippines and the United States.[151] Eleanor Funda (now Funda-Sardual) was the wartime baby whose parents the Sillimans had befriended while hiding from the Japanese in mountains. Her father, Joaquin Funda, worked with Bob in the resistance.[152] Eleanor also graduated from Silliman University, also earned a Master's Degree in American and English Literature, later taught at the University, ran a family fish farm, and became a member of the Municipal Council in Ipil on the island of Mindanao, south of Negros in the Philippines.[153] Frederick S. Dael, born in 1947, came to the Sillimans at age 6. He was extremely bright and later graduated from Silliman University. A

self-made man, he became a very successful corporate manager, former
president of Pepsi Cola for the Far East, former chairman of Islacom,
managing director of CEO's Inc. and Chairman of the Board of Silliman
University. He was awarded the Outstanding Sillimarian Award by the
University in 1995.[154]

FIGURE 40.
Emma Cole [Teves], 1953, Herbert H. and Grace A. Dow Family Papers, Courtesy of
The Herbert H. and Grace A. Dow Foundation.

FIGURE 41.
Eleanor Funda [-Sardual], 1960, Silliman Collection #68, Courtesy of The Herbert H. and Grace A. Dow Foundation.

FIGURE 42.
Metta Silliman with Frederick S. Dael, 1956, Silliman Collection #68, Courtesy of The Herbert H. and Grace A. Dow Foundation.

Metta tutored the children in English, the Bible, and other subjects
while Bob taught math and geography. The Sillimans were strict but
fair with the children. Their daughter Emma commented,

> Living with them was wonderful. Sundays were always
> special, we would all go to church together and then
> after the service we'd have special Sunday luncheon. In
> the afternoon after everybody had a nap or just quiet
> time reading, my dad would say 'how about all of us
> go for a ride to Camp Lookout' or 'how about we go to
> Silliman farm beach and go for a swim or sometimes he
> and I would go biking round the city.[155]

The Sillimans received help for the education of the children from
members of the Memorial Presbyterian Church in Midland, and
from the E. O. Barstow Scholarship fund set up by a member of the
church.[156]

§§§

By the end of the 1960s, Silliman University had become one of
the preeminent universities of Asia. The school had done much
to cement Filipino-American friendship on a person-to-person level
through its mission work, extension services, and community projects.
The graduates of the university could be found in all major professions
in the Philippines, including congressional representatives, senators,
governmental department heads, judges, lawyers, doctors, and man-
agers in business, agriculture, and industry. Their mission then was
to "mold and develop our young people through a program of education for responsible citizenship, for purposeful living, and for creative
thinking."[157]

On Founders Day in 1963— also the sixty-second anniversary of the
school— the Sillimans received certificates of recognition for their contributions to Silliman University.[158] When they decided to retire in
1966, the city of Dumaguete named them adopted son and daughter

of the city and accorded them all the rights and privileges of citizenship.[159] They were additionally honored by the Filipino press and by university President Dr. Cicero D. Calderon.

FIGURE 43.
Silliman University President Cicero D. Calderon recognizing Robert and Metta Silliman at their retirement celebration, 1966, with Governor Agustin Perdices at far left, Silliman Collection #68, Courtesy of The Herbert H. and Grace A. Dow Foundation.

When they left the Philippines in September 1966, five hundred people attended the airport send-off, including Governor Perdices, the Mayor, the Provincial Judge, the Catholic priests and the Mother Superior, the entire Silliman University faculty, and even the Silliman Band. The airline pilots also got into the act by flying over the city and circling the campus so the Sillimans could have one last look at their beloved second homeland.[160]

§§§

Back in the United States, Metta and Bob Silliman and Metta's sister Abby retired to southern California and lived out their remaining years, first in Pasadena and then at the Westminster Presbyterian retirement facility in Duarte, California just east of Pasadena.

FIGURE 44.
At their retirement in 1966, the Silliman received accolades for their work at Silliman University from the Filipino press which celebrated their contribution along with Silliman University Founder David Hibbard and his wife Laura shown together in a caricature by D. Aguila in the *Asia Newsweekly Examiner,* August 28, 1966, Silliman Collection #68, Courtesy of The Herbert H. and Grace A. Dow Foundation and Courtesy of Dani Aguila.

FIGURE 45.
Robert and Metta Silliman near their
retirement, c 1960s, Silliman Collection
#68, Courtesy of The Herbert H. and
Grace A. Dow Foundation.

FIGURE 46.
Robert Silliman shakes hands with Governor Agustin Perdices on departure from
Dumaguete, 1966, Courtesy of Frederick S. Dael.

Still considering the Sillimans "their" missionaries, the Women's Association
of the Memorial Presbyterian church continued some minimal support (a
few hundred dollars per year) for them well into their retirement.[161] It was
not an easy retirement due to Metta's poor health and growing dementia[162]
from Parkinson's disease, but they were able to share a common interest

and experience with their Presbyterian colleagues at Westminster, many of whom had also been church missionaries around the world.[163] Bob remained actively involved in finding funds for Silliman students and even published a detailed account of Filipino-American guerrilla activities on Negros during the war, a book that he had started while still in the Philippines.[164] Abby died in 1983. Metta died in 1988, and Robert survived until 1990.[165]

FIGURE 47.
Westminster Gardens, a Presbyterian retirement community in Duarte, California where the Sillimans and Abby Jacobs lived out their remaining years, brochure, 1960s, Silliman Collection #68, Courtesy of The Westminster Gardens and Courtesy of The Herbert H. and Grace A. Dow Foundation.

FIGURE 48.
Westminster Gardens, a Presbyterian retirement community in Duarte, California
where the Sillimans and Abby Jacobs lived out their remaining years, postcard,
1960s, Silliman Collection #68, Courtesy of The Westminster Gardens and Courtesy of
The Herbert H. and Grace A. Dow Foundation.

§§§

In the 1940s, about halfway through their missionary career, the average term of service for a Presbyterian Foreign Missionary was twelve years. By their retirement in 1966, the Sillimans had served over forty years of missionary work in the Philippines. Through their mission, Robert and Metta Silliman taught thousands of students and stood witness to their faith during years of personal trials.

They believed their work in the Philippines at Silliman University was made possible by the constant encouragement and support of Grace Dow and the Presbyterian Church in Midland.[166] Grace Dow gained tremendously from this relationship not only by continuing her service to others, but also by sharing the lives of people who had committed so fully to their faith. Her financial support also helped educate Silliman University students, many of whom went on to become national leaders in many fields.

FIGURE 49.
Metta and Robert Silliman in California, March 14, 1969, Silliman Collection #68,
Courtesy of The Herbert H. and Grace A. Dow Foundation.

Although Silliman University's relationship with the national
Presbyterian Church has transformed into a wider ecumenical approach,
dedication to the original Christian underpinnings of the college
has allowed it to persevere through some difficult times, especially
when the university was shut down temporarily in the 1970s by the
President Ferdinand Marcos administration. The University stayed
true to its roots and showed that its interest was in helping students
grow to become responsible, purposeful, and creative citizens helping
make the Philippines a talented, diverse, and vibrant country today.

The First Presbyterian Church, renamed The Bertha E. R. Strosacker
Memorial Presbyterian Church when they moved into their new struc-
ture in 1953, had supported the Robert and Metta Silliman for decades
and had been able to share in their mission work in the Philippines.
The close relationship with the Sillimans gave the members of the
church a tangible sense of what they could do to impact the lives of
others, not only through supporting the Silliman's religious mission

but also by providing much needed goods to those in need and offering scholarships to Silliman University students.

The collaboration of the church, the missionaries, the patron, and the university allowed tremendous contributions to each of their communities that were impossible in isolation.

What a wonderful legacy of service for them all.[167]

ABOUT THE AUTHOR

Tawny Ryan Nelb

Tawny Ryan Nelb is an archivist and historian based in Midland, Michigan.

Ms Nelb was born in Kentucky and raised in several states before settling in Mishawaka in the South Bend, Indiana area with her family. She attended the University of Notre Dame and received a BA in American Studies in 1975 as one of the first classes of women at the university. She worked for the Herbert Hoover Presidential Library in West Branch, Iowa and then for ten years for the Yale University Manuscript and Archives Department.

In 1983, Tawny obtained her MA in American History. She became an independent archival consultant/historian in 1986, and in 1989, she moved her consulting business, Nelb Archival Consulting, Inc. (www.nelbarchival.com), to Midland, MI. She has provided recommendations for archival management and preservation of historical and vital records for clients all over the country including the Houston Museum of Fine Arts, the Archives of Michigan, UCLA, Rollin M. Gerstacker Foundation, Independence National Historic Park in Philadelphia, Alden B. Dow Archives, Cal Poly in San Luis Obispo, CA, the University of Texas at Austin, and the Rock and Roll Hall of Fame in Cleveland, Ohio, among many others.

Ms Nelb has written over 40 articles and three books on historical records preservation and history topics, including *The Pines: 100 Years of the Herbert H. and Grace A. Dow Homestead, Orchards, and Gardens*, and *A Cultural Incubator: The Post Street Schoolhouse from 1888-Present*. Her book on archival architectural records, *Architectural Records: Managing Design and Construction Records*, co-authored with Waverly Lowell, won the Waldo Gifford Leland award in 2007 from the Society of American Archivists for "writing of superior excellence and usefulness in the field of archival history, theory, or practice." She lectures several times a year on local history and archival practices.

Ms Nelb is a past president of the Historical Society of Michigan, a past member of the Executive Board for the Midland Center for the Arts and of the Advisory Board of the Midland County Historical Society, and sits on the Governor's Michigan State Historical Records Advisory Board. In 2011, she was among the many women honored for their contributions in their fields in the *Voices: Extraordinary Women of Midland County* exhibit at the Doan Center of the Midland County Historical Society and the Midland Center for the Arts.

2012

§§§

Footnotes

1   Minnie [Warner] Ball, *First Presbyterian Church of Midland, 1867-1947*, Midland, MI: McKay Press, 1948, 5; Genealogical Notations, Ball Family Bible, Ball Family Series, Herbert H. and Grace A. Dow Family Papers, Herbert H. and Grace A. Dow Foundation, Midland, MI.

2   Ball, 9, 29; Register of Communicants, *Church Register*, Book I, 1867-1945, Memorial Presbyterian Church Archives, Midland, MI.

3   Dorothy Langdon Yates, *The Memorial Presbyterian Church: Our Centennial Year 1867-1967*, Midland, MI: McKay Press, 1967, 29; Herbert and Grace separately pledged to the church a total of $700 or the equivalent of about $8,600 in today's money. First Presbyterian Church Pledges, April 1, 1925 to April 1, 1926, Financial Records 1926, Memorial Presbyterian Church Archives, Midland, MI; Inflation Calculator, http://www.westegg.com/inflation/, accessed September 15, 2011.

4   Osborn Dow would have attended church with his parents but he did not become an official member due to his death in 1902 at age 2 ½.

5   Abbey Circle Records, 1921-1982; Missionary Society Records, 1895-1950, Memorial Presbyterian Church Archives, Midland, MI.

6   Missionary Society Records, 1895-1950, Memorial Presbyterian Church Archives, Midland, MI.

7   Yates, 44.

8   Yates, 44.

9   "Rev. V. V. Nicholas to Resign After 20 Years of Service, *Midland Republican*," 25 April 1935; Notes on the Sillimans, c 1977, Box 2, Folder 4, Collection 68, Herbert H. and Grace A. Dow Foundation, Midland, MI; Robert Silliman to Dear Midland Friends, July 13, 1953, Box 2, Folder 2, Collection #68, Herbert H. and Grace A. Dow Family Papers, Herbert H. and Grace A. Dow Foundation, Midland, MI.

10   Contribution Notes, 1925 Income Tax Return, Financial Series, Herbert H. and Grace A. Dow Family Papers, Herbert H. and Grace A. Dow Foundation, Midland, MI; Inflation Calculator, http://www.westegg.com/inflation/, accessed September 15, 2011.

11   Notes from telephone conversation to Manila, Philippines with Fred Dael (the Silliman's foster son) and the author, March 2001.

12   Metta Jacobs Archer Silliman, Personnel Records, 1924-1967, Record Group 360, Presbyterian Historical Society, Philadelphia, PA; U.S. Federal Census Records, Detroit, MI, 1900; Fred Dael annotation added to booklet draft text, December 2008.

13   Horace B. Silliman was already known for his generosity in funding a new church building for his local Presbyterian congregation and a building at Hamilton College in Utica, New York and would later provide funds for buildings at Union College in Schenectady, New York and Mount Herman School in East Northfield, Massachusetts among others. "Mr. Silliman's Generous Gift," *New York Times*, 3 May 1889; "Gift for a Church in Cohoes," *New York Times*, 28 June 1895; "Dr. H. B. Silliman's Gift," *New York Times*, 21 May 1901: "Gift to Mt. Hermon School," *New York Times*, 18 August 1902.

14   "Silliman: Gates of Opportunity," Pamphlet, c 1959-1960, Box 2, Folder 11, Collection #68, Herbert H. and Grace A. Dow Foundation, Midland, MI.

15   Horace B. Silliman later gave another $70,000 to Silliman University. Antonio S. Gabila, "Silliman University: America's

Gift to the Philippines," *Silliman Alumni Bulletin*, August-December, 1963, 3, Box 1, Folder 11, Collection #68, Herbert H. and Grace A. Dow Foundation, Midland, MI.

16 Dr. Hibbard and his wife Laura Crooks Hibbard would raise their family in Dumaguete, teach students, and remain at Silliman Institute until near retirement age. Anne C. Kwantes, *Presbyterian Missionaries in the Philippines: Conduits of Social Change (1899-1910)*, Quezon City, Philippines: New Day Publishers, 1989, 132.

17 Pronounced doo-mah-geh-teh.

18 Edilberto K. Tiempo, Crispin C. Maslog, T. Valentino Sitoy, Jr., *Silliman University: 1901-1976*, Dumaguete City, Philippines: Silliman University Press, 1977, 4, Memorial Presbyterian Church Library, Midland, MI.

19 Tiempo, 7.

20 Tiempo, 10; Charles A. Gunn, *Presbyterian Church and the Philippines*, New York: Board of Foreign Missions of the Presbyterian Church in the USA, 1913, 16.

21 Kwantes, 134.

22 Silliman Institute became a University in 1938. Antonio S. Gabila, "Silliman University: America's Gift to the Philippines," *Silliman Alumni Bulletin*, August-December, 1963, 4, Box 1, Folder 11, Collection #68, Herbert H. and Grace A. Dow Foundation, Midland, MI.

23 Belle M. King, "A Close-Up of the Philippine Missions," *Women and Missions* Magazine, c 1933, 94-96, Box 10, Folder 115, Herbert H. and Grace A. Dow Family Papers, Herbert H. and Grace A. Dow Foundation, Midland, MI; Tiempo, 6.

24 King, 95.

25 Kwantes, 121.

26 Leon O. Ty, "The Magnificent Americans," *The Asia Newsweekly Examiner*, August 28, 1966, Box 2, Folder 9, Silliman Collection #68, Herbert H. and Grace A. Dow Foundation, Midland, MI.

27 Attributed to Dorothy Wilson, Notes on Robert and Metta Jacobs Silliman, c 1986, Box 2, Folder 4, Silliman Collection #68, Herbert H. and Grace A. Dow Foundation, Midland, MI; Robert Benton Silliman, Personnel Records, 1926-1967, Record

Group 360, Presbyterian Historical Society, Philadelphia, PA; Leon O. Ty, "The Magnificent Americans," *The Examiner*, August 28, 1966, Box 2, Folder 9, Silliman Collection #68, Herbert H. and Grace A. Dow Foundation, Midland, MI; Robert B. Silliman, *Pocket of Resistance: Guerrilla Warfare in Negros Island*, Philippines, Manila, Philippines: Philippines Editions, 1980, end flyleaf; Robert B. Silliman Oral History, July 18, 1983, RG MSC272. C958, Presbyterian Historical Society, Philadelphia, PA.

28   Yates, 45; Notes on Contributions, Income Tax Return 1927, Restricted Financial Series, Herbert H. and Grace A. Dow Family Papers, Midland, MI.

29   Grace kept her support of the Sillimans quiet even in her reports to the Missionary Society in 1930 where she makes no mention of them. Grace Dow report for the Woman's Missionary Society, Financial Records, 1930, Memorial Presbyterian Church Archives, Midland, MI.

30   Yates, viii.

31   "How to Follow Christ and Win Others to Do So," Enclosure in letter, Robert B. Silliman, February 4, 1934, Box 10, Folder 116, Herbert H. and Grace A. Dow Family Papers, Herbert H. and Grace A. Dow Foundation, Midland, MI.

32   Donald K. McKim, *Presbyterian Beliefs*, Louisville, KY: Geneva Press, 2003, 108.

33   Unfortunately, Grace Dow's letters to the Sillimans did not survive after the war.

34   Robert Silliman to Grace Dow, April 11, 1951, Box 12, Folder 148, Herbert H. and Grace A. Dow Family Papers, Herbert H. and Grace A. Dow Foundation, Midland, MI for letter about the personal nature of their correspondence.

35   In fact, Metta and her sister Abby R. Jacobs, who came to Silliman University later, became the backbone of the English department. Abby started what later became the Speech and Theatre Department and the college of Performing Arts. Steven Trent Smith, *The Rescue: The True Story of Courage and Survival in World War II*, New York: John Wiley & Sons, Inc., 2001, 15; Fred Dael annotations added to text draft, December 2008.

36   King, 94-96.

37 Roy H. Brown, President of Silliman Institute to Grace Dow, September 4, 1933, Box 12, Folder 154, Herbert H. and Grace A. Dow Family Papers, Herbert H. and Grace A. Dow Foundation, Midland, MI.

38 Robert Silliman to Grace Dow, September 24, 1933, Box 10, Folder 115, Herbert H. and Grace A. Dow Family Papers, Herbert H. and Grace A. Dow Foundation, Midland, MI.

39 Robert Silliman to Grace Dow, September 24, 1933, Box 10, Folder 115, Herbert H. and Grace A. Dow Family Papers, Herbert H. and Grace A. Dow Foundation, Midland, MI.

40 Bob Silliman to Grace Dow, September 24, 1933, Box 10, Folder 115, Herbert H. and Grace A. Dow Family Papers, Herbert H. and Grace A. Dow Foundation, Midland, MI.

41 Robert Silliman to Grace Dow, May 10, 1933, Box 10, Folder 115, Herbert H. and Grace A. Dow Family Papers, Herbert H. and Grace A. Dow Foundation, Midland, MI.

42 Inflation Calculator, http://www.westegg.com/inflation/, accessed September 15, 2011.

43 Bank Account Summaries including checks to Robert and Metta Silliman, 1935-1953, Financial Records, Herbert H. and Grace A. Dow Family Papers, Herbert H. and Grace A. Dow Foundation, Midland, MI.

44 Robert Silliman to Grace Dow, September 24, 1933, Box 10, Folder 115, Herbert H. and Grace A. Dow Family Papers, Herbert H. and Grace A. Dow Foundation, Midland, MI; Roy H. Brown, President of Silliman Institute to Grace Dow, September 4, 1933, Box 12, Folder 154, Herbert H. and Grace A. Dow Family Papers, Herbert H. and Grace A. Dow Foundation, Midland, MI; Robert Silliman to John Gardner, August 23, 1953, Box 1, Folder 4, Collection #68, Herbert H. and Grace A. Dow Family Papers, Herbert H. and Grace A. Dow Foundation, Midland, MI.

45 Robert Silliman to Grace Dow, May 1, 1941, Box 10, Folder 125, Herbert H. and Grace A. Dow Family Papers, Herbert H. and Grace A. Dow Foundation, Midland, MI.

46 Metta Silliman to Uncle Tom Coleman, January 7, 1936, Box 2, Folder 1, Silliman Collection #68, Herbert H. and Grace A. Dow Foundation, Midland, MI; Frances B. Cogan, *Captured: The*

Japanese Internment of American Civilians in the Philippines, 1941-1945, Athens, GA: University of Georgia Press, 2000, 87.

47   According to their son, Fred Dael, this Christmas gift giving became a ritual until 1967. Fred Dael annotation of draft text, December 2008.

48   Abby R. Jacobs was born on March 4, 1904 in Detroit, Michigan. She attended Western College and the University of Illinois for her undergraduate degree and then taught high school in Waverly, Illinois, Benton Harbor, Michigan, and Ottumwa, Iowa before applying to the Presbyterian Church for missionary service. She was appointed in March 2, 1931 and sailed for the Philippines in April 24, 1931. She taught English and speech classes at Silliman Institute. After her escape from Negros during the war (see: story in main text) she served on General Douglas McArthur's staff writing radio scripts in Australia and returned to the Philippines to serve as a program director of a post-war military radio station in Manila. In 1946, she resumed work with the Presbyterian Board of Foreign Missions as part of the Division of Education and Information in radio research. She retired in 1968. Her own wartime story is told in her autobiographical monograph, *We Did Not Surrender,* published that same year. Personnel Records, 1931-1959, Record Group 360, Presbyterian Historical Society, Philadelphia, PA.

49   Metta Silliman to Uncle Tom Coleman, January 7, 1936, Box 2, Folder 1, Silliman Collection #68, Herbert H. and Grace A. Dow Foundation, Midland, MI.

50   Yates, 57.

51   Robert Silliman annotation on letter, Metta Silliman to Uncle Tom Coleman, January 7, 1936, Box 2, Folder 1, Silliman Collection #68, Herbert H. and Grace A. Dow Foundation, Midland, MI.

52   Robert Silliman to Grace Dow, January 1, 1940, Box 10, Folder 119, Herbert H. and Grace A. Dow Family Papers, Herbert H. and Grace A. Dow Foundation, Midland, MI; Metta and Bob Silliman, January 5, 1940, Box 10, Folder 119, Herbert H. and Grace A. Dow Family Papers, Herbert H. and Grace A. Dow Foundation, Midland, MI.

53   Luzon, one will remember, is the island location of Bataan and Corregidor fame from World War II where thousands of American and Filipino soldiers died. Bob and his son Fred repeated this trip together years later to visit the tomb of the famous American Anthropologist Henry Otley Beyer who died in 1966. Fred Dael annotations on draft text, December 2008.

54   Robert Silliman to Grace Dow, April 25, 1934, Box 10, Folder 117, Herbert H. and Grace A. Dow Family Papers, Herbert H. and Grace A. Dow Foundation, Midland, MI.

55   Tiempo, 30.

56   *Dumaguete Station Quarterly Newsletter*, September 1938, Box 1, Folder 10, Silliman Collection #68, Herbert H. and Grace A. Dow Foundation, Midland, MI.

57   Lafayette College in Easton, Pennsylvania awarded Robert Silliman an honorary doctorate in 1956. Fred Dael annotations on draft text, December 2008.

58   "Society Hears Talk of Philippine Work," *Midland Daily News,* 23 September 1937.

59   Co. Roy M. Stanley II, *Prelude to Pearl Harbor: War in China, 1937-41 Japan's Rehearsal for World War II*, New York: Charles Scribner's Sons, 1982.

60   Metta Silliman to Grace Dow, August 11, 1940, Box 10, Folder 121, Herbert H. and Grace A. Dow Family Papers, Herbert H. and Grace A. Dow Foundation, Midland, MI.

61   Hitler invaded Poland in September 1939, Belgium in May 1940, The Netherlands in May 1940, and France in May 1940.

62   Metta Silliman to Grace Dow, August 11, 1940, Box 10, Folder 121, Herbert H. and Grace A. Dow, Family Papers, Herbert H. and Grace A. Dow Foundation, Midland, MI.

63   Robert Silliman to Grace Dow, September 28, 1940, Box 10, Folder 121, Herbert H. and Grace A. Dow Family Papers, Herbert H. and Grace A. Dow Foundation, Midland, MI.

64   Robert Silliman to Grace Dow, February 9, 1941, Box 10, Folder 124, Herbert H. and Grace A. Dow Family Papers, Herbert H. and Grace A. Dow Foundation, Midland, MI.

65   Metta Silliman to Grace Dow, January 4, 1941, Box 10, Folder 124, Herbert H. and Grace A. Dow Family Papers, Herbert H. and

Grace A. Dow Foundation, Midland, MI; "3,000,000 Pesos Fire Razes Center of Dumaguete," February 4, 1941, Box 10, Folder 124, Herbert H. and Grace A. Dow Family Papers, Midland, MI; Robert Silliman to Grace Dow, February 9, 1941, Box 10, Folder 124, Herbert H. and Grace A. Dow Family Papers, Herbert H. and Grace A. Dow Foundation, Midland, MI.

66 Metta Silliman to Grace Dow, March 9, 1941, Box 10, Folder 124, Herbert H. and Grace A. Dow Family Papers, Herbert H. and Grace A. Dow Foundation, Midland, MI.

67 Robert Silliman to Grace Dow, March 2, 1941, Box 10, Folder 124, Herbert H. and Grace A. Dow Family Papers, Midland, Michigan; "Americans Called to Meet Today to Organize Coordinating Committee," enclosure in Robert Silliman to Grace Dow, March 2, 1941, Box 10, Folder 121, Herbert H. and Grace A. Dow Family Papers, Herbert H. and Grace A. Dow Foundation, Midland, MI.

68 Newspaper articles with European and Pacific war news in the local Midland press and newspapers across the country, U. S. military service conscription beginning in October 1940, increased United States defense spending, and nationwide calls to rearm, certainly alerted most people in the United States to the inevitability of war. "FDR Asks 'Total Defense' Promises U. S. Will Shun War," *Midland Daily News,* 10 July 1940; "Tell Registration Plans," *Midland Daily News,* 10 October 1940; See also: *Midland Daily News*, 1937-1941, Grace A. Dow Library, Midland, MI.

69 Metta Silliman to Grace Dow, May 9, 1941, Box 10, Folder 125, Herbert H. and Grace A. Dow Family Papers, Herbert H. and Grace A. Dow Foundation, Midland, MI.

70 Robert Silliman to Grace Dow, May 1, 1941, Box 10, Folder 125, Herbert H. and Grace A. Dow Family Papers, Herbert H. and Grace A. Dow Foundation, Midland, MI.

71 Robert Silliman to Grace Dow, May 1, 1941, Box 10, Folder 125, Herbert H. and Grace A. Dow Family Papers, Herbert H. and Grace A. Dow Foundation, Midland, MI.

72 Robert Silliman to Grace Dow, May 9, 1941, Box 10, Folder 125, Herbert H. and Grace A. Dow Family Papers, Herbert H. and Grace A. Dow Foundation, Midland, MI.

73 Robert Silliman to Grace Dow, June 8, 1941, Box 10, Folder 125, Herbert H. and Grace A. Dow Family Papers, Herbert H. and Grace A. Dow Foundation, Midland, MI.

74 Robert Silliman to Grace Dow, July 27, 1941, Box 10, Folder 125, Herbert H. and Grace A. Dow Family Papers, Herbert H. and Grace A. Dow Foundation, Midland, MI.

75 Metta Silliman to Grace Dow, August 10, 1941, Box 10, Folder 126, Herbert H. and Grace A. Dow Family Papers, Herbert H. and Grace A. Dow Foundation, Midland, MI.

76 Metta Silliman to Grace Dow, August 10, 1941, Box 10, Folder 126, Herbert H. and Grace A. Dow Family Papers, Herbert H. and Grace A. Dow Foundation, Midland, MI.

77 Robert Silliman to Grace Dow, October 13, 1941, Box 10, Folder 126, Herbert H. and Grace A. Dow Family Papers, Herbert H. and Grace A. Dow Foundation, Midland, MI. A letter was sent from Mrs. H. M. Wenger to Mrs. C. N. Morrison, January 17, 1942 concerning the shipment of a box of clothing to the Sillimans but it is unlikely either ever arrived. *Missionary Society Annual Report*, 1942, Memorial Presbyterian Church Archives, Midland, MI; The Sillimans sent their last cable to the U.S. presumably to family in February 1942 with the words, "Safe, Well. Optimistic." Abby Jacobs, *We Did Not Surrender*, Manila, Philippines, privately printed, 1986, 65, Silliman Collection #68, Herbert H. and Grace A. Dow Foundation, Midland, MI.

78 Jacobs, 3.

79 "Philippines under Attack, Say Japs Landed," *Midland Daily News,* 9 December 1941; "Repulse Luzon Invasion," *Midland Daily News,* 10 December 1941; Jacobs, 10; Silliman, *Pocket of Resistance*, 4.

80 Scott A. Mills, *Stranded in the Philippines: Professor Bell's Private War Against the Japanese*, Annapolis, MD: Naval Institute Press, 2009, 12.

81 Silliman, *Pocket of Resistance*, 5, 41.

82 Jacobs, 12.

83 Jacobs, 18; Silliman, *Pocket of Resistance*, 23.

84 Jacobs, 63, Silliman, *Pocket of Resistance*, 52; Mills, 36.

85   The Board of Foreign Missions of the Presbyterian Church in the
      United States Station Letter, October 1944, Box 11, Folder 127,
      Herbert H. and Grace A. Dow Family Papers, Herbert H. and
      Grace A. Dow Foundation, Midland, MI.

86   For more on the evasion from capture and internment or work
      with the guerrillas of other the Silliman University faculty fami-
      lies during World War II see: Frances B. Cogan, *Captured: The
      Japanese Internment of American Civilians in the Philippines, 1941-
      1945*, Athens, GA: University of Georgia Press, 2000 and Steven
      Trent Smith, *The Rescue: The True Story of Courage and Survival in
      World War II*, New York: John Wiley & Sons, Inc., 2001; Scott
      A. Mills, *Stranded in the Philippines: Professor Bell's Private War
      Against the Japanese*, Annapolis, MD: Naval Institute Press, 2009;
      Arthur L. Carson, *Silliman University: 1901-1959*, New York,
      NY: United Board for Christian Education in Asia, 1965.

87   Silliman, *Pocket of Resistance*, 90.

88   Mills, 17.

89   Jacobs, 62; Silliman, *Pocket of Resistance*, 239.

90   Jacobs, 55.

91   Jacobs, 61, Silliman, *Pocket of Resistance*, 239.

92   "Three-Minute Lead on Japs Too Close Says Silliman," *Midland
      Daily News,* 24 March 1945.

93   Jacobs, 122-124.

94   Robert Silliman Oral History, Presbyterian Historical Society.
      At the same time, Mrs. MacArthur asked her husband about
      the Sillimans, he was reading reports about Bob's activities.
      MacArthur directed his wife to let Bob's mother know they were
      alive but cautioned secrecy. There is no evidence this information
      was passed on to the members of the First Presbyterian Church or
      to Grace Dow.

95   National Archives and Records Administration, World War
      II Prisoners of War, 1941-1946 [database on-line], Provo, UT,
      USA: The Generations Network, Inc. 2005. Original Data,
      World War II Prisoners of War Data File [Archival Database],
      Records of World War II Prisoners of War, 1942-1947, Records
      of the Office of the Provost Marshal General, Record Group 389,
      National Archives at College Park, College Park, MD.

96 "Three-Minute Lead on Japs Too Close Says Silliman," *Midland Daily News,* 24 March 1945.

97 Jacobs, 60, 74, 77-95.

98 Silliman, *Pocket of Resistance,* 145; Mills, 33, 59.

99 Silliman, *Pocket of Resistance,* 220.

100 The Island of Negros was divided into two provinces which follow the geographical division of the mountains on the island and the two different ethnolinguistic groups: The northern section is called Negros Occidental and the southern section is called Negros Oriental.

101 Silliman, *Pocket of Resistance,* 219; Mills, 127; Speech Delivered by the City Mayor on the Occasion of the Testimonial Dinner in Honor of Dr. and Mrs. Silliman, May 23, 1966, Box 2, Folder 6, Silliman Collection #68, Herbert H. and Grace A. Dow Foundation, Midland, MI.

102 Silliman, *Pocket of Resistance,* 238, 251.

103 Silliman, *Pocket of Resistance,* 245, 251, 262; Jacobs, 119; Dorothy Wilson, "Robert and Metta Silliman," 1961, Box 2, Folder 5, Herbert H. and Grace A. Dow Family Papers, Herbert H. and Grace A. Dow Foundation, Midland, MI.

104 Silliman, *Pocket of Resistance,* 314.

105 Silliman, *Pocket of Resistance,* 283.

106 Silliman, *Pocket of Resistance,* 289.

107 Silliman, *Pocket of Resistance,* 297-299, Mills, 156.

108 The Board of Foreign Missions of the Presbyterian Church in the United States Station Letter, October 1944, Box 11, Folder 127, Herbert H. and Grace A. Dow Family Papers, Herbert H. and Grace A. Dow Foundation, Midland, MI.

109 Silliman, *Pocket of Resistance,* 290-291.

110 Silliman, *Pocket of Resistance,* 296.

111 Mills, 158.

112 Silliman, *Pocket of Resistance,* 290-291.

113 Jacobs, 126-128.

114 Jim Christley and Tony Bryan, *U. S. Submarines, 1941-1945,* Westminster, MD: Osprey Publishers, 2006, 5; David Hinkle, *United States Submarines,* New York, NY: Universe, 2002, 110.

115 Jacobs, 132; Mills, 158; Silliman, *Pocket of Resistance*, 311; Arthur L. Carson, *Silliman University: 1901-1959*, New York, NY: United Board for Christian Education in Asia, 1965, 250-251. Additional families from Silliman University were rescued in May 1944 via the submarine, U.S.S. *Crevalle*. Smith, 209.

116 Jacobs, 134; Mills, 159.

117 Mills, 161-162.

118 "Sillimans to Resume Teaching Jobs at Presbyterian School in Philippines," *Midland Daily News*, 7 May 1946.

119 Robert Silliman to Grace Dow, June 29, 1944, Box 11, Folder 127, Herbert H. and Grace A. Dow Family Papers, Herbert H. and Grace A. Dow Foundation, Midland, MI; Robert Silliman to Grace Dow, August 12, 1944, Box 11, Folder 127, Herbert H. and Grace A. Dow Family Papers, Herbert H. and Grace A. Dow Foundation, Midland, MI; Fred Dael commented his mother suffered with pain from this injury for the rest of her life. Fred Dael, annotations on draft text sent to author, December 11, 2008.

120 Robert Silliman to Grace Dow, August 12, 1944, Box 11, Folder 127, Herbert H. and Grace A. Dow Family Papers, Herbert H. and Grace A. Dow Foundation, Midland, MI; Robert Silliman to Grace Dow, September 24, 1944, Box 1, Folder 4, Silliman Collection #68, Herbert H. and Grace A. Dow Foundation, Midland, MI.

121 Metta Silliman to Grace Dow, September 14, 1944, Box 11, Folder 127, Herbert H. and Grace A. Dow Family Papers, Herbert H. and Grace A. Dow Foundation, Midland, MI.

122 Robert Silliman to Grace Dow, September 14, 1944, Box 1, Folder 4, Silliman Collection #68, Herbert H. and Grace A. Dow Foundation, Midland, MI.

123 Silliman, *Pocket of Resistance*, 79.

124 Robert Silliman to Grace Dow, September 14, 1944, Box 1, Folder 4, Silliman Collection #68, Herbert H. and Grace A. Dow Foundation, Midland, MI; Silliman Library Committee to Friends, February 7, 1945, Women's Federation Annual Report, 1945, Memorial Presbyterian Church Archives, Midland, MI.

125 Dorothy Wilson, "Notes on the Sillimans," nd, Box 2, Folder 4, Silliman Collection #68, Herbert H. and Grace A. Dow Foundation, Midland, MI.

126 Robert Silliman to John Gardner, February 4, 1945, Box 1, Folder 4, Silliman Collection #68, Herbert H. and Grace A. Dow Foundation, Midland, MI; For information on the Japanese internment of American civilians see: Frances B. Cogan, *Captured: The Japanese Internment of American Civilians in the Philippines, 1941-1945*, Athens, GA: University of Georgia Press, 2000.

127 Robert Silliman to Grace Dow, October 22, 1944, Box 11, Folder 127, Herbert H. and Grace A. Dow Family Papers, Herbert H. and Grace A. Dow Foundation, Midland, MI.

128 Metta Silliman to Grace Dow, May 21, 1945, Box 11, Folder 128, Herbert H. and Grace A. Dow Family Papers, Herbert H. and Grace A. Dow Foundation, Midland, MI.

129 John Gardner to Robert Silliman, February 8, 1945, Box 1, Folder 5, Silliman Collection #68, Herbert H. and Grace A. Dow Foundation, Midland, MI; "Church Groups to Hear Talks by Teachers of Silliman University," *Midland Daily News,* 19 March 1945; "Three-Minute Lead on Japs Too Close, Says Silliman," *Midland Daily News,* 24 March 1945.

130 John Gardner to Robert Silliman, February 20, 1945, Box 1, Folder 4, Silliman Collection #68, Herbert H. and Grace A. Dow Foundation, Midland, MI.

131 "Three-Minute Lead on Japs Too Close Says Silliman," *Midland Daily News,* 24 March 1945.

132 Robert Silliman to Grace Dow, May 8, 1945, Box 11, Folder 128, Herbert H. and Grace A. Dow Family Papers, Herbert H. and Grace A. Dow Foundation, Midland, MI; Robert Silliman to Grace Dow, June 24, 1945, Box 11, Folder 129, Herbert H. and Grace A. Dow Family Papers, Herbert H. and Grace A. Dow Foundation, Midland, MI; Robert Benton Silliman, Personnel Records, 1926-1967, Record Group 360, Presbyterian Historical Society, Philadelphia, PA. Grace Dow also gave the Silliman's each 70 shares of Dow Chemical Company stock in late 1952 before her death. Robert Silliman to Grace Dow, October 19, 1952, Box 12, Folder 151 and Robert Silliman to Grace Dow, Feb

1, 1953, Herbert H. and Grace A. Dow Family Papers, Herbert H. and Grace A. Dow Foundation, Midland, MI.

133 "Sillimans to Resume Teaching Jobs at Presbyterian School in Philippines," *Midland Daily News,* 7 May 1946, Robert Silliman Oral History, Presbyterian Historical Society, 5.

134 Silliman, *Pocket of Resistance,* 51; "The Gates of Silliman Reopen," *Silliman University Newsletter,* No. 4, Jul 1945, Box 1, Folder 19, Collection 68, Silliman Collection #68, Herbert H. and Grace A. Dow Foundation, Midland, MI.

135 Metta Silliman to Grace Dow, August 7, 1946, Box 1, Folder 3, Silliman Collection #68, Herbert H. and Grace A. Dow Foundation, Midland, MI.

136 Metta and Robert Silliman to Dear Friends, September 11, 1946, Box 1, Folder 6, Collection 68, Herbert H. and Grace A. Dow Foundation.

137 Dorothy Wilson to Mr. and Mrs. Silliman, October 16, 1949, Box 2, Folder 1, Silliman Collection #68, Herbert H. and Grace A. Dow Foundation, Midland, MI.

138 "A Bit of MPC [Memorial Presbyterian Church] History for Your Summer Reading: the Sillimans Who Are They?" c 1980s, Box 2, Folder 6, Silliman Collection #68, Herbert H. and Grace A. Dow Foundation, Midland, MI; Lists of material sent to the Sillimans, 1940-50s, Box 2, Folder 7, Silliman Collection #68, Herbert H. and Grace A. Dow Foundation, Midland, MI.

139 Dorothy Wilson to Leopoldo T. Ruiz, July 2, 1949, Box 2, Folder 1, Silliman Collection #68, Herbert H. and Grace A. Dow Foundation, Midland, MI.

140 Dorothy Wilson, "Notes on the Sillimans," no date, Box 2, Folder 4, Silliman Collection #68, Herbert H. and Grace A. Dow Foundation, Midland, MI.

141 Robert Silliman to Grace Dow, June 18, 1950, Box 12, Folder 146, Herbert H. and Grace A. Dow Family Papers, Herbert H. and Grace A. Dow Foundation, Midland, MI.

142 Robert Benton Silliman, Personnel Records, 1926-1967, Record Group 360, Presbyterian Historical Society, Philadelphia, PA; Robert and Metta Silliman in Chronological Roll of

Communicants, *Church Register*, Book II, January 6, 1951, Memorial Presbyterian Church Archives, Midland, MI.

143 "Visit of Robert and Metta Silliman Our Two Missionaries," John Gardner to the Congregation, c January 1951, Box 1, Folder 6, Silliman Collection #68, Herbert H. and Grace A. Dow Foundation, Midland, MI.

144 Robert Silliman to Grace Dow, November 3, 1952, Box 12, Folder 151, Herbert H. and Grace A. Dow Family Papers, Herbert H. and Grace A. Dow Foundation, Midland, MI.

145 Antonio S. Gabila, "Silliman University: America's Gift to the Philippines," *Silliman Alumni Bulletin*, August-December, 1963, 4, Box 1, Folder 11, Silliman Collection #68, Herbert H. and Grace A. Dow Foundation, Midland, MI.

146 Metta Silliman to Grace Dow, August 11, 1940, Box 10, Folder 121, Herbert H. and Grace A. Dow Family Papers, Herbert H. and Grace A. Dow Foundation, Midland, MI.

147 Robert Silliman to Midland Friends, July 13, 1953, Box 2, Folder 2, Silliman Collection #68, Herbert H. and Grace A. Dow Foundation, Midland, MI.

148 Metta Silliman to Grace Dow, February 19, 1951, Box 12, Folder 147, Herbert H. and Grace A. Dow Family Papers, Herbert H. and Grace A. Dow Foundation, Midland, MI.

149 Robert Silliman to Grace Dow, April 11, 1951, Box 12, Folder 148, Herbert H. and Grace A. Dow Family Papers, Herbert H. and Grace A. Dow Foundation, Midland, MI.

150 Metta Silliman to Grace Dow, January 16, 1934, Box 10, Folder 116 and Metta Silliman to Grace Dow, March 23, 1952, Box 12, Folder 150, Herbert H. and Grace A. Dow Family Papers, Herbert H. and Grace A. Dow Foundation, Midland, MI.

151 Emma Cole married Eduardo C. Teves, and they have two children. Emma Cole Teves letter to the author, September 6, 2008 and November 6, 2008.

152 Photograph, Outstanding Sillimanian Award, 1995, Courtesy Fred S. Dael; Emma Cole Teves to the Author, September 6, 2008; Mills, 155, 167.

153 Eleanor Funda-Sardual is married and has three children. She is extremely grateful for the Silliman's emphasis on education in the

household. Their counsel helped her develop a disciplined focus and goal for her studies. Eleanor Funda-Sardual to the Author, January 1, 2010.

154   Fred Dael annotations to author on draft text, December 11, 2008; "Foundation University Admits New Corporate Members," Dumaguete Metro Post, http://dumaguete metropost.com/fu-admits-new-corporate-members-p362-85.htm, accessed September 17, 2011.

155   Emma Cole Teves letter to the author, September 3, 2008.

156   Yates, 45.

157   Dr. Cicero D. Calderon, "Silliman University and Its Mission,", *Silliman Alumni Bulletin*, August-December, 1963, 6, Silliman Collection #68, Herbert H. and Grace A. Dow Foundation, Midland, MI; In 1972, the university survived imposition of martial law by President Ferdinand Marcos that shut down all the universities in the country. Today Silliman University's mission remains rooted in their past but looks to their future. They consider themselves a leading Christian institution committed to total human development for the well-being of society and the environment. Tiempo, 198, 201-202, 209; Silliman University Mission and Vision Statement, Silliman University, http://www.su.edu.ph/general_info/ mission.html, accessed September 15, 2011.

158   "The Sixty-Second Anniversary," *Silliman Alumni Bulletin*, August-December, 1963, 9, Silliman Collection #68, Herbert H. and Grace A. Dow Foundation, Midland, MI.

159   Robert Silliman to Grace Dow, April 11, 1951, Box 12, Folder 148, Herbert H. and Grace A. Dow Family Papers, Herbert H. and Grace A. Dow Foundation, Midland, MI.

160   Robert Silliman to Dorothy Wilson, October 6, 1966, Box 2, Folder 9, Silliman Collection #68, Herbert H. and Grace A. Dow Foundation, Midland, MI.

161   Proposed Budget 1986, Women's Association, Memorial Presbyterian Church, Box 2, Folder 6, Silliman Collection #68, Herbert H. and Grace A. Dow Foundation, Midland, MI.

162 Robert Silliman to Dorothy Wilson, October 15, 1979, Box 2, Folder 4, Silliman Collection #68, Herbert H. and Grace A. Dow Foundation, Midland, MI.

163 Westminster Gardens Brochure, c 1970s, Box 2, Folder 9, Silliman Collection #68, Herbert H. and Grace A. Dow Foundation, Midland, MI.

164 Robert B. Silliman, *Pocket of Resistance: Guerrilla Warfare in Negros Island*, Philippines, Manila, Philippines: Philippines Editions, 1980.

165 Social Security Death Index, Ancestry.com, http://search.ancestry.com/search/db.aspx?dbid=3693, accessed September 15, 2011.

166 Robert Silliman to Grace Dow, October 22, 1944, Box 11, Folder 127, Herbert H. and Grace A. Dow Family Papers, Herbert H. and Grace A. Dow Foundation, Midland, MI.

167 In recognition of their service to Silliman University, in August 2008, a new multimedia center was named Robert and Metta Silliman Hall in their honor. Emma Cole Teves, Dedication Speech, August 26, 2008.

INDEX

Black and white illustrations are indicated by *ill* after the page number.

Page numbers including an "n" indicate an endnote on that page.